My First Book about the Alphabet of Fish

Amazing Animal Books Children's Picture Books

By Molly Davidson

Mendon Cottage Books

JD-Biz Publishing

Read More Amazing Animal Books

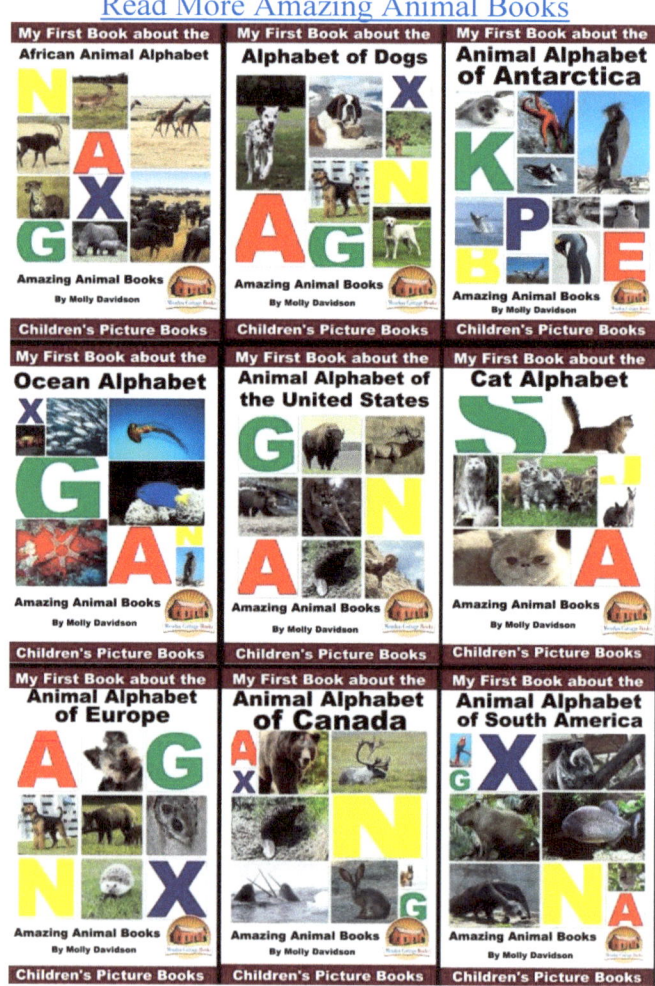

Purchase at Amazon.com

Download Free Books!

http://MendonCottageBooks.com

Introduction

All fish has a spinal cord, gills (which they use to breath the oxygen out of the water), and they are covered in scales.

Fish have a small brain when compared to other animals.

A is for an Arawana.

The Arawana fish lives in freshwater rivers in northern South America.

They grow to be about 4 feet long and weigh around 20 pounds.

It can jump over 3 feet out of the water to catch prey in the trees along the river bank.

 **is also for an Atlantic Cod.**

The Atlantic Cod lives in the depths of the ocean from Greenland south to North Carolina.

Cod eat plants and animals, like herring, eels, moss, sprats, and some cod have been caught with interesting items in their stomachs like an oil cans or clothes.

 **is for Bass.**

Bass are the number freshwater fish fished for in the World.

They're very smart and will only get tricked by a fisherman's hook once, then they know every other time to avoid it, since it is dangerous.

The boy bass is in charge of protecting the eggs once the girl has laid them.

C is for a Catfish.

Catfish are found swimming in freshwater all over the World, except in Antarctica.

Their whiskers, called barbels, are used for smelling, which helps them find food.

They lay between 10 - 90 eggs, each time, which hatch in less than one week.

C is also for a Carp.

Carp live in the freshwater of North and South America, Asia, New Zealand, Australia, Africa, and Europe.

They are closely related to goldfish and buffalo fish.

D is for a Dolphinfish.

Dolphinfish are found in warm and tropical seas around the World.

They are one of the most colorful fish in the sea, with a green and yellow body and a blue long dorsal (top) fin.

E is for an Eel.

Eels can be anywhere between 5 - 13 feet long.

They have a slimy mucus covering which protects them from getting scratched on the coral reef, where they live.

They usually live about 85 years.

F

is for a Flounder.

Flounder are found mostly in the shallow ocean waters from Maine to South Carolina.

They are a flat fish that usually blend in with the ocean floor.

To help confuse their predators they have several dark spots on their body, which look like eyes.

G is for a Grouper.

Grouper are a species of brightly colored sea bass found in tropical seas.

Some grouper fish can weigh up to 800 pounds and be 8 feet long.

G is also for a Gar.

Gar fish swim in the freshwaters of North and Central America.

They are an aggressive fish, and only have a few predators, like alligators, crocodiles, and humans.

 **is for Halibut.**

Halibut are a large flat fish that live on the sandy bottoms of the ocean floor.

They mainly eat food as it drifts on the ocean floor, like crustaceans, squid, mollusks, and shrimp.

I is for an Icefish.

Icefish live in the icy cold ocean water around Antarctica.

They have clear blood and white gills.

They eat krill, plankton, and smaller fish.

 **is for a Jack.**

Jack fish live in the tropical waters of the Indian, Atlantic, and Pacific Oceans.

Most species of jack weigh between 30 - 50 pounds.

 **is for a Kokanee.**

Kokanee, also called sockeye salmon, live in Russia, Japan, British Columbia, the Yukon, Alaska, Washington, Oregon, and Idaho.

The boys turn from silver to red when it is spawning, also called mating, time.

L is for a Leerfish.

The leerfish lives in the Atlantic Ocean around the coasts of North America and Africa, also into the Mediterranean Sea.

They grow to be around 4 1/2 feet long, weighing around 40 pounds.

L is also for a Lutjaniche, the scientific name for a Snapper.

Snappers live in the Gulf of Mexico, north along the Atlantic Ocean coast to New York.

They swim mostly around the coral reefs, down to ocean depths of around 300 feet.

They like to swim in groups, called schools, as well as by themselves.

M is for a Marlin.

Marlin can be found in the tropical Atlantic, Pacific, and Indian Oceans.

They are very aggressive and like to defend their territory.

M is also for Mackerels.

Mackerels are part of the family which includes Albacore, tuna, and Bonito fish.

They travel in large groups, called schools.

 **is for a Nembwe.**

Frederick Hermanus Can der Bank © <u>Wikimedia Commons</u>

Nembwe are found in southern Africa, in Lake Malawi and the Shire River.

This fish is very similar to the American Bass, both in appearance and actions.

 **is for an Oscar.**

Oscar fish live in the Orinocok Amazon and La Plata River basins in South America, as well as in Florida, Puerto Rico, Hawaii, Guam, the Ivory Coast, and Hong Kong.

They are a strong fish, even though they only weigh about 3 1/2 pounds.

P is for a Pink Salmon.

Pink salmon are found in rivers from Washington north to Alaska and into the northwest Canadian territories.

They live in the ocean for the first 18 months of life, then swim upstream to lay their eggs, then they die after only 2 years of life.

P is also for a Piranha.

Piranhas have lived in the coastal rivers of South America for over 25 million years.

They have razor sharp teeth, but they aren't really man eaters, they mainly eat seeds, dead fish, worms, crustaceans, insects, and plants.

 **is for a Queen Parrotfish.**

Queen parrotfish live in the coral reefs in the Caribbean Sea.

They use their beaks to scrape plants and algae from the surface of the coral.

These fish are all born as girls, but as they grow the larger fish become boys.

 is for a Rainbow Trout.

Rainbow trout are found in rivers and lakes from the west coast of North America east to the Rocky Mountains.

They are cousins to the salmon.

R is also for a Rockfish.

Rockfish are a large group of several species of fish, which live and hide in deep of the ocean around the rocks.

They come in all different colors, lengths, and sizes.

 **is for Sharks.**

There are 465 different species of sharks living in all the World's Oceans.

Sharks have been around since before the dinosaurs.

Most sharks hunt in the evening and at night.

T is for a Tuna.

Tuna are a saltwater fish, living in most of the Earth's Oceans.

There are 15 different species of tuna.

The word tuna comes from the Latin word *thunnus*, which means to rush or dart along.

T is also for Triggerfish.

Triggerfish are a brightly colored species which live in the tropical oceans around the World.

They are very aggressive and protective of their territory; they are known to bite scuba divers, not because they look like food, but just to protect their space.

 **is for a Warmouth.**

Fredlyfish4 © <u>Wikimedia Commons</u>

Warmouth live in the Great Lakes and Mississippi River of North America down to the Gulf of Mexico.

They live in the weed covered, muddy bottoms of lakes and rivers.

Warmouth fish have teeth on their tongues.

 is for an X-Ray Tetra.

X-Ray Tetra are a small fish that is native to the Amazon River in South America, and is also a popular aquarium fish

Their scales are translucent, clear, making it very easy to see their spine; this is why they are called an x-ray fish.

 **is for a Yellowtail.**

Yellowtails live in the coastal waters around California, Brazil, Argentina, South Africa, Australia, and New Zealand.

They are fast swimmers; swimming over 40 mph, at times.

 **is for a Zander.**

The Zander fish can be found in lakes and rivers in Finland, Sweden, and western Asia.

They live in the weed beds in small schools.

Zander hunt for food around dawn and dusk, and rest in between feedings.

Conclusion

I hope you have enjoyed reading about the many different and amazing fish.

One more fact; there are over 30,000 different species of fish living in the World today.

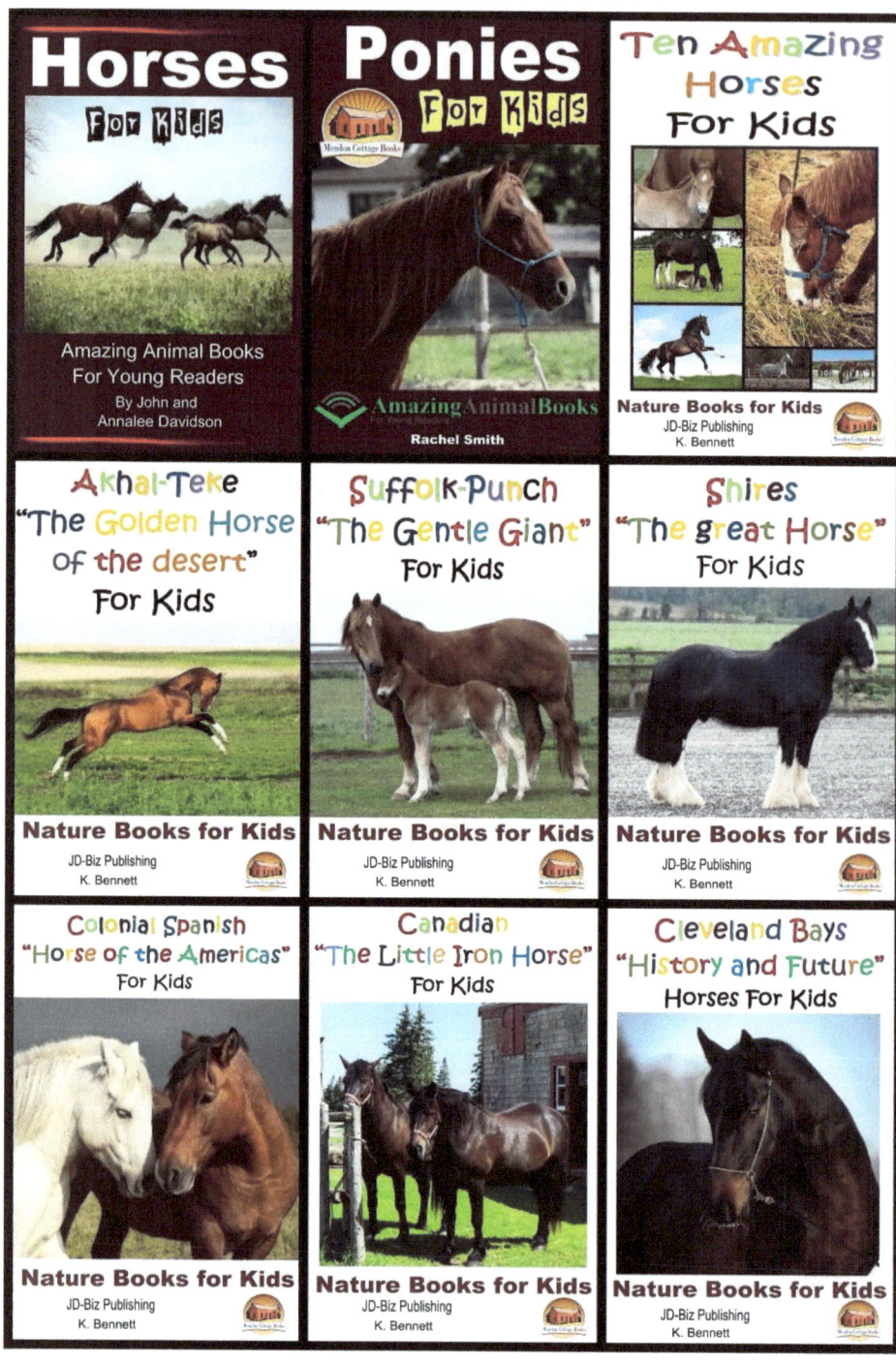

Our books are available at

1. Amazon.com

2. Barnes and Noble

3. Itunes

4. Kobo

5. Smashwords

6. Google Play Books

Download Free Books!
http://MendonCottageBooks.com

Publisher

JD-Biz Corp

P O Box 374

Mendon, Utah 84325

http://www.jd-biz.com/

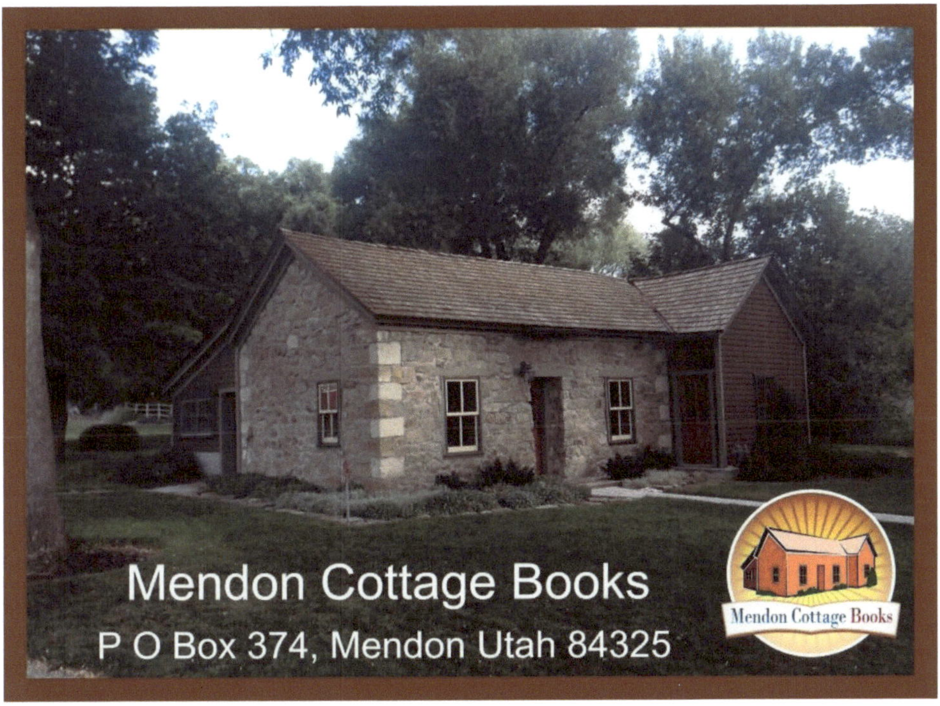

Mendon Cottage Books

P O Box 374, Mendon Utah 84325